Can't Feel My Face, Renegades & More Hot Singles

ISBN 978-1-4950-4930-9

HAL•LEONARD®
CORPORATION
7777 W. BLUEMOUND RD. P.O. BOX 13819 MILWAUKEE, WI 53213

Visit Hal Leonard Online at
www.halleonard.com

Can't Feel My Face

Words and Music by Abel Tesfaye, Max Martin, Savan Kotecha, Ali Payami and Peter Svensson

2

Renegades

Words and Music by Alexander Junior Grant, Adam Levin, Casey Harris, Noah Feldshuh and Sam Harris

Capo II

Key of Bm (Capo Key of Am)

Intro

Moderately slow, in 2

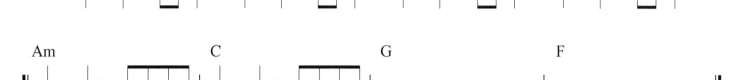

Verse

Am   C   G   F

1. Run a-way - ee - ay with me, (Da, da, da.   Da, da, da.   Da, da, da.)
2. Long live the pi - o - neers,

Am   C   G   F

lost souls in rev-el - ry. (Hey! Da, da, da.   Da, da, da.   Da, da, da.)
reb - els and mu-ti- neers.

Am   C   G   F

Run-nin' wild and run-nin' free. (Da, da, da.   Da, da, da.   Da, da, da.)
Go forth and have no fear.

Am   C   G   F

Two kids, you and me. (Hey! Da, da, da.   Da, da, da.)   And I say, hey,
Come close and lend an ear.

𝄉 Chorus

Am   C   G   F

hey, hey, hey, liv- in' like we're ren - e - gades.   Hey, hey, hey,

Am   C   G   F

hey, hey, hey, liv- in' like we're ren - e - gades,   ren - e - gades,

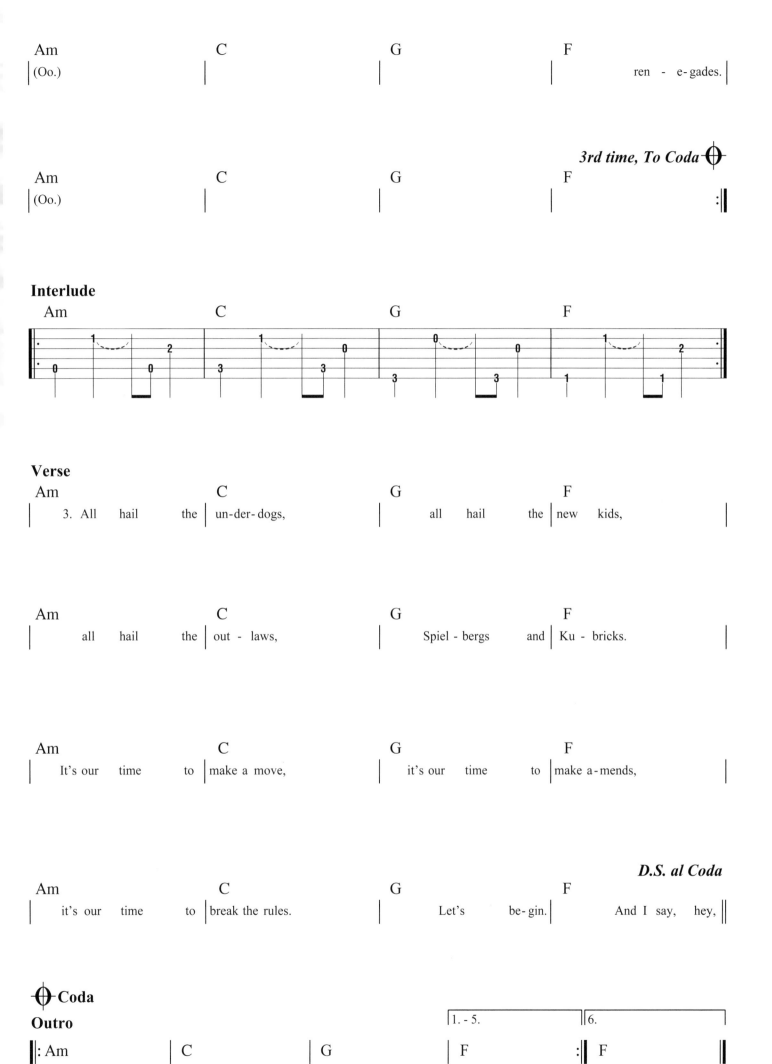

Shut Up and Dance

Words and Music by Ryan McMahon, Ben Berger, Sean Waugaman,
Eli Maiman, Nicholas Petricca and Kevin Ray

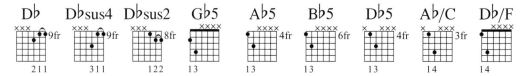

Key of Db

Intro

Moderately fast

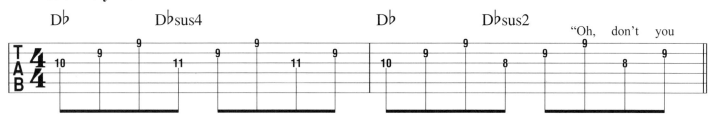

"Oh, don't you

§ Chorus

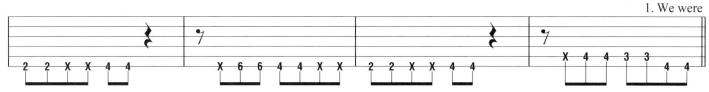

dare look back, just keep your | eyes on me." I said,"You're | hold-in' back."She said,"Shut | up and dance with me."

This wom-an is my | des-ti-ny. She said, | "Oo, hoo. Shut | up and dance with me."

Interlude

Verse

Pre-Chorus

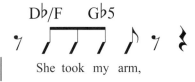 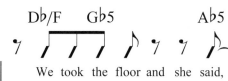

She took my arm, | I don't know how it hap-pened. | We took the floor and she said,

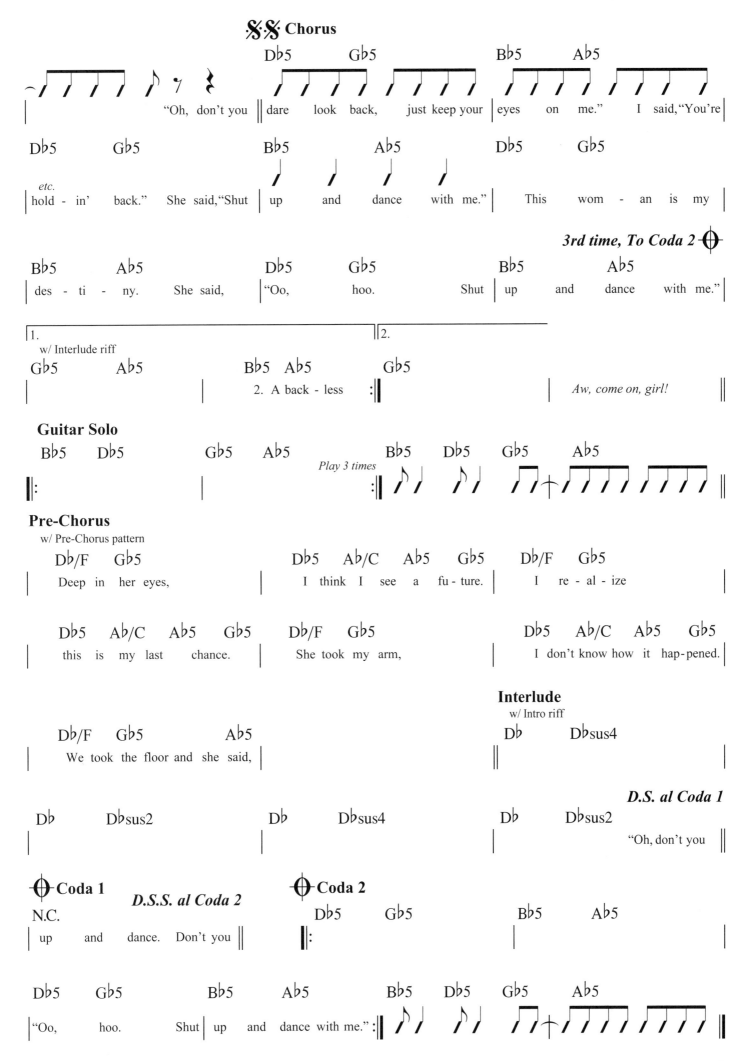

Tear in My Heart

Words and Music by Tyler Joseph

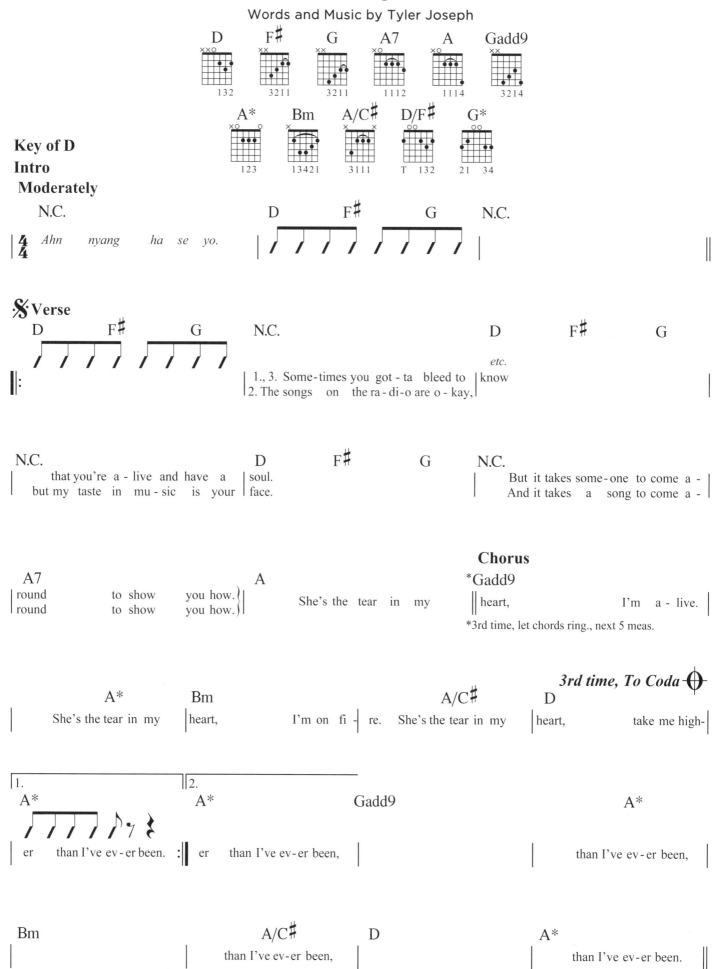

Key of D
Intro
Moderately

N.C.

| D F♯ | G | N.C.

4/4 *Ahn nyang ha se yo.*

%Verse

D F♯ | G | N.C. | D F♯ G | *etc.*

1., 3. Some-times you got-ta bleed to know
2. The songs on the ra-di-o are o-kay,

N.C. | D F♯ G | N.C.

that you're a-live and have a soul. But it takes some-one to come a-
but my taste in mu-sic is your face. And it takes a song to come a-

A7 | A | **Chorus** *Gadd9

round to show you how. She's the tear in my heart, I'm a-live.
round to show you how.

*3rd time, let chords ring., next 5 meas.

3rd time, To Coda ⊕

A* Bm | A/C♯ D

She's the tear in my heart, I'm on fi-re. She's the tear in my heart, take me high-

1.
A* | er than I've ev-er been.

2.
A* Gadd9 | A*
er than I've ev-er been, than I've ev-er been,

Bm | A/C♯ D | A*
than I've ev-er been, than I've ev-er been.

Bridge

$(\museighthnote\musequarternote = \musequarternote\museighthnote^{3})$

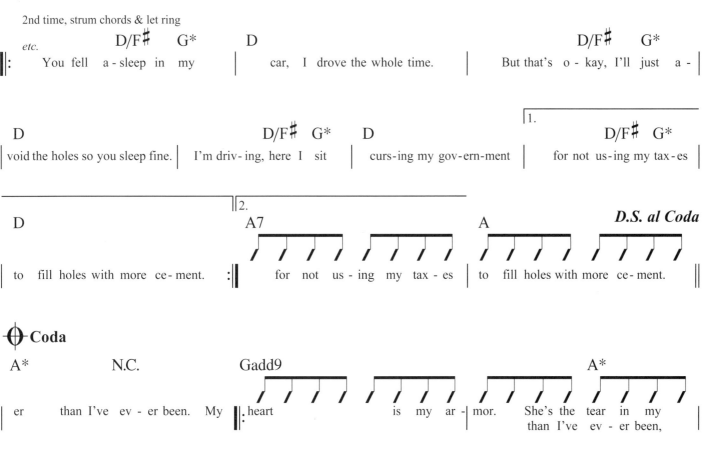

D   D/F#   G*   D

(Oh,   oh,   oh,   oh.   Oo,   oo,   oo,   oo.)

2nd time, strum chords & let ring

etc.   D/F#   G*   D   D/F#   G*

You fell a-sleep in my | car, I drove the whole time. | But that's o-kay, I'll just a-

D   D/F#   G*   D   **1.**   D/F#   G*

void the holes so you sleep fine. | I'm driv-ing, here I sit | curs-ing my gov-ern-ment | for not us-ing my tax-es

D   **2.**   A7   A   ***D.S. al Coda***

to fill holes with more ce-ment. | for not us-ing my tax-es | to fill holes with more ce-ment.

⊕ Coda

A*   N.C.   Gadd9   A*

er   than I've ev-er been. My | heart   is my ar-| mor.   She's the tear in my
                                                                 than I've ev-er been,

Bm   A/C#   D

etc.
heart,   she's a carv-| er.   She's a butch-er with a | smile,   cut me far-
                                   than I've ev-er been,   oh,

1.   **2.**   **Outro-Chorus**

A*   A*   *G*

- ther than I've ev-er been, | than I've ev-er been. My | heart   is my ar-
                                                       Let chords ring till end.

A*   Bm   A/C#

mor.   She's the tear in my | heart,   she's a carv-| er.   She's a butch-er with a

Freely

D   A*   D

smile,   cut me far | - ther   than I've | ev-er been.

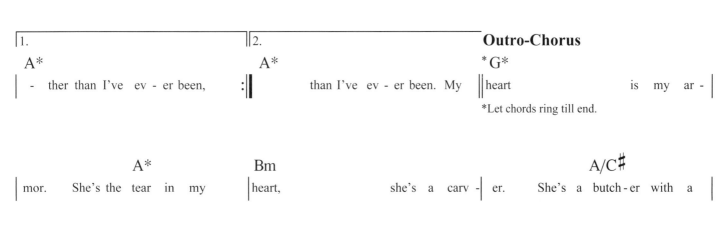

Uma Thurman

Words and Music by Andrew Hurley, Joseph Trohman, Patrick Stump, Peter Wentz,
Jacob Scott Sinclair, Liam O'Donnell, Waqaas Hashmi, Jarrell Young, Jack Marshall and Bob Mosher

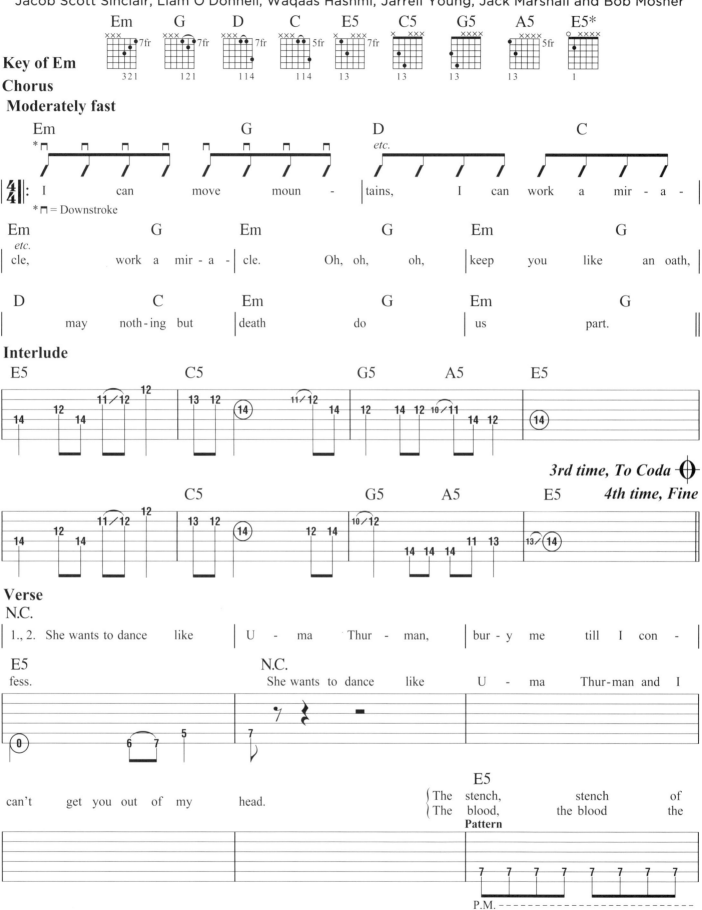

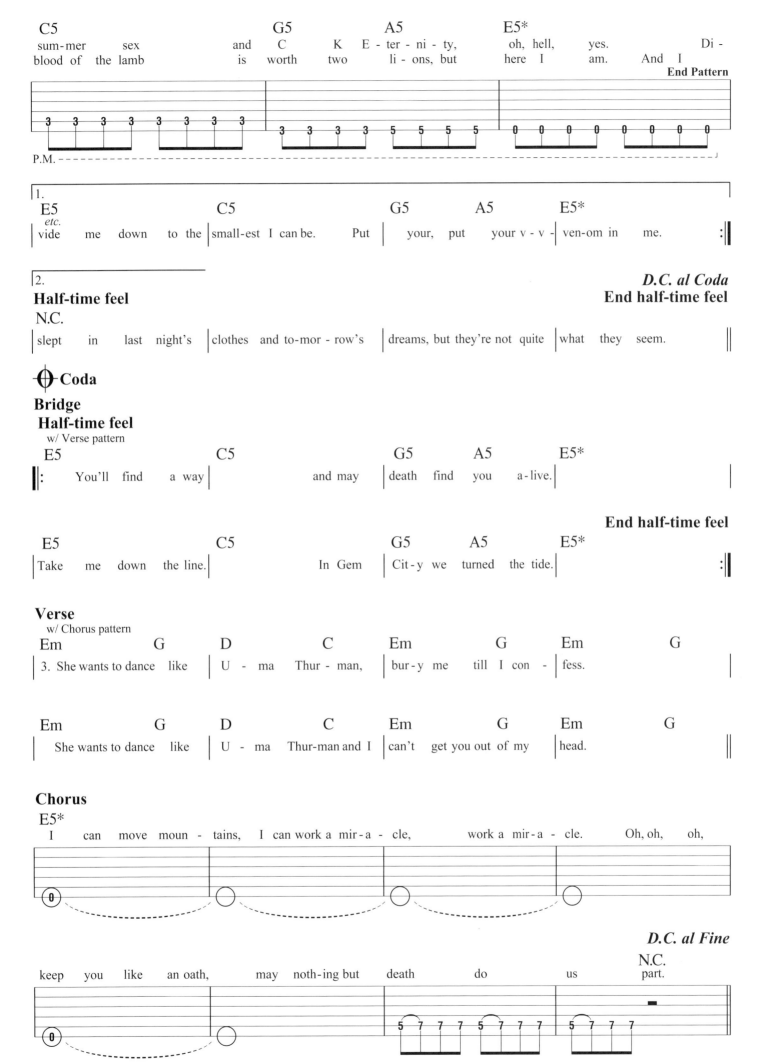

C5   G5   A5   E5*

sum-mer sex   and   C   K   E - ter - ni - ty,   oh, hell,   yes.   Di -

blood of the lamb   is   worth   two   li - ons, but   here I   am.   And I

End Pattern

P.M. -

1.

E5   C5   G5   A5   E5*

etc.

vide   me   down   to the   small-est I can be.   Put   your, put   your v - v - ven-om   in   me.

2.

D.C. al Coda

Half-time feel   **End half-time feel**

N.C.

slept   in   last   night's   clothes and to-mor - row's   dreams, but they're not quite   what   they   seem.

⊕ Coda

Bridge
Half-time feel

w/ Verse pattern

E5   C5   G5   A5   E5*

‖:   You'll   find   a way   and may   death   find   you   a-live.

End half-time feel

E5   C5   G5   A5   E5*

Take   me   down   the line.   In Gem   Cit - y   we   turned   the tide.   :‖

Verse
w/ Chorus pattern

Em   G   D   C   Em   G   Em   G

3. She wants to dance   like | U - ma   Thur - man, | bur-y me   till I con - | fess.

Em   G   D   C   Em   G   Em   G

She wants to dance   like | U - ma   Thur-man and I | can't   get you out of my | head.

Chorus

E5*

I   can   move   moun - tains,   I can work a mir-a-cle,   work a mir-a-cle.   Oh, oh,   oh,

D.C. al Fine

N.C.

keep   you   like   an oath,   may   noth-ing but   death   do   us   part.

Rhythm Tab Legend

Rhythm Tab is a form of notation that adds rhythmic values to the traditional tab staff.

TABLATURE graphically represents the guitar fingerboard. Each horizontal line represents a string, and each number represents a fret. Rhythmic values are shown using ovals, stems, and dots.

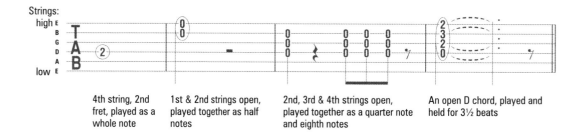

4th string, 2nd fret, played as a whole note

1st & 2nd strings open, played together as half notes

2nd, 3rd & 4th strings open, played together as a quarter note and eighth notes

An open D chord, played and held for 3½ beats

Definitions for Special Guitar Notation

HALF-STEP BEND: Strike the note and bend up 1/2 step.

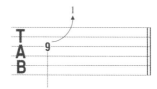

WHOLE-STEP BEND: Strike the note and bend up one step.

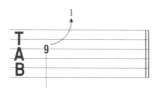

QUARTER-STEP BEND: Strike the note and bend up 1/4 step.

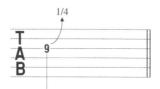

BEND AND RELEASE: Strike the note and bend up as indicated, then release back to the original note. Only the first note is struck.

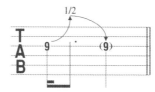

PRE-BEND: Bend the note as indicated, then strike it.

VIBRATO: The string is vibrated by rapidly bending and releasing the note with the fretting hand.

HAMMER-ON: Strike the first (lower) note with one finger, then sound the higher note (on the same string) with another finger by fretting it without picking.

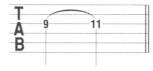

PULL-OFF: Place both fingers on the notes to be sounded. Strike the first note, and without picking, pull the finger off to sound the second (lower) note.

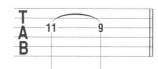

LEGATO SLIDE: Strike the first note and then slide the same fret-hand finger up or down to the second note. The second note is not struck.

SHIFT SLIDE: Same as legato slide, except the second note is struck.

GRACE-NOTE SLUR: Strike the note and immediately hammer-on (pull-off or slide) as indicated.

TRILL: Very rapidly alternate between the notes indicated by continuously hammering on and pulling off.

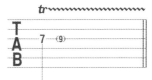

NATURAL HARMONIC: Strike the note while the fret hand lightly touches the string directly over the fret indicated.

Harm.

MUFFLED STRINGS: A percussive sound is produced by laying the fret hand across the string(s) without depressing, and striking them with the pick hand.

PALM MUTING: The note is partially muted by the pick hand lightly touching the string(s) just before the bridge.

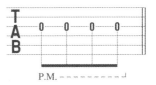

P.M. ------------

Additional Musical Definitions

3	*(staccato)*	• Play the note short	
3	*(fermata)*	• A hold or pause	
⊓		• Downstroke	
V		• Upstroke	
D.S. al Coda		• Go back to the sign (%), then play until the measure marked *"To Coda,"* then skip to the section labelled *"Coda."*	
D.C. al Fine		• Go back to the beginning of the song and play until the measure marked *"Fine"* (end).	

Rhy. Fig. • Label used to recall a recurring accompaniment pattern (usually chordal).

Riff • Label used to recall composed, melodic lines (usually single notes) which recur.

N.C. • No chord

tacet • Instrument is silent (drops out).

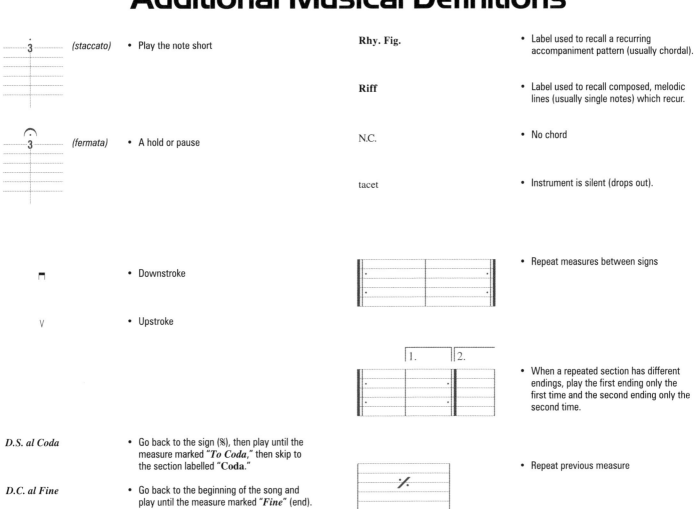

• Repeat measures between signs

• When a repeated section has different endings, play the first ending only the first time and the second ending only the second time.

• Repeat previous measure

• Repeat previous two measures

NOTE: Tablature numbers in parentheses are used when:
- The note is sustained, but a new articulation begins (such as a hammer-on, pull-off, slide, or bend), or
- A bend is released.

HAL LEONARD GUITAR CHEAT SHEETS

The Hal Leonard Cheat Sheets series includes lyrics, chord frames, and "rhythm tab" (cut-to-the-chase notation) to make playing easier than ever! No music reading is required, and all the songs are presented on two-page spreads to avoid page turns.

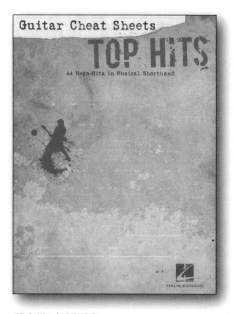

TOP HITS

44 pop favorites, including: Are You Gonna Be My Girl • Baby • Bad Day • Bubbly • Clocks • Crazy • Fireflies • Gives You Hell • Hey, Soul Sister • How to Save a Life • I Gotta Feeling • Just the Way You Are • Lucky • Mercy • Mr. Brightside • Need You Now • Take Me Out • Toes • Use Somebody • Viva La Vida • You Belong with Me • and more.
00701646 ....$14.99

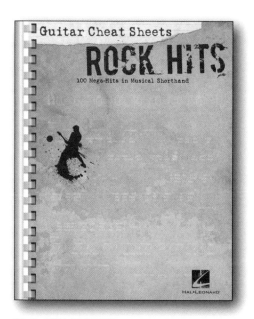

ROCK HITS

44 songs, including: Are You Gonna Go My Way • Black Hole Sun • Counting Blue Cars • Float On • Friday I'm in Love • Gives You Hell • Grenade • Jeremy • Kryptonite • Push • Scar Tissue • Semi-Charmed Life • Smells like Teen Spirit • Smooth • Thnks Fr Th Mmrs • Two Princes • Use Somebody • Viva La Vida • Where Is the Love • You Oughta Know • and more.
00702392 ....$24.99

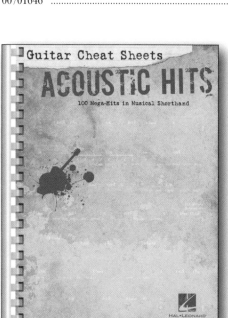

ACOUSTIC HITS

100 unplugged megahits in musical shorthand: All Apologies • Crazy Little Thing Called Love • Creep • Daughter • Every Rose Has Its Thorn • Hallelujah • I'm Yours • The Lazy Song • Little Lion Man • Love Story • More Than Words • Patience • Strong Enough • 21 Guns • Wanted Dead or Alive • Wonderwall • and more.
00702391 ....$24.99

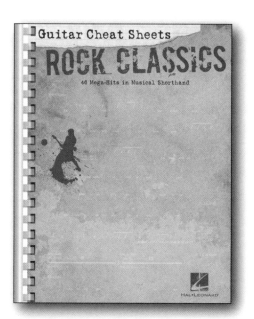

ROCK CLASSICS

Nearly 50 classics, including: All Right Now • Barracuda • Born to Be Wild • Carry on Wayward Son • Cat Scratch Fever • Free Ride • Layla • Message in a Bottle • Paranoid • Proud Mary • Rhiannon • Rock and Roll All Nite • Slow Ride • Smoke on the Water • Sweet Home Alabama • Welcome to the Jungle • You Shook Me All Night Long • and more.
00702393 ....$24.99

HAL•LEONARD® CORPORATION

7777 W. BLUEMOUND RD. P.O. BOX 13819 MILWAUKEE, WI 53213

Visit Hal Leonard online at **www.halleonard.com**

Prices, contents, and availability subject to change without notice. 0712

THE BOOK SERIES
FOR EASY GUITAR

THE ACOUSTIC BOOK
00702251 Easy Guitar $16.99

THE BEATLES BOOK
00699266 Easy Guitar $19.95

THE BLUES BOOK – 2ND ED.
00702104 Easy Guitar $16.95

THE CHRISTMAS CAROLS BOOK
00702186 Easy Guitar $14.95

THE CHRISTMAS CLASSICS BOOK
00702200 Easy Guitar $14.95

THE ERIC CLAPTON BOOK
00702056 Easy Guitar $18.95

THE CLASSIC COUNTRY BOOK
00702018 Easy Guitar $19.95

THE CLASSIC ROCK BOOK
00698977 Easy Guitar $19.95

THE CONTEMPORARY CHRISTIAN BOOK
00702195 Easy Guitar $16.95

THE COUNTRY CLASSIC FAVORITES BOOK
00702238 Easy Guitar $19.99

THE DISNEY SONGS BOOK
00702168 Easy Guitar $19.95

THE FOLKSONGS BOOK
00702180 Easy Guitar $14.95

THE GOSPEL SONGS BOOK
00702157 Easy Guitar $15.95

THE HYMN BOOK
00702142 Easy Guitar $14.99

THE LOVE SONGS BOOK
00702064 Easy Guitar $16.95

THE NEW COUNTRY HITS BOOK
00702017 Easy Guitar $19.95

THE ELVIS BOOK
00702163 Easy Guitar $19.95

THE ROCK CLASSICS BOOK
00702055 Easy Guitar $18.95

THE WEDDING SONGS BOOK
00702167 Easy Guitar $16.95

THE WORSHIP BOOK
00702247 Easy Guitar $14.99

FOR MORE INFORMATION, SEE YOUR LOCAL MUSIC DEALER,
OR WRITE TO:

www.halleonard.com

Prices, contents, and availablilty subject
to change without notice.

Disney characters and artwork © Disney Enterprises, Inc.

HAL•LEONARD®
CORPORATION
7777 W. BLUEMOUND RD. P.O. BOX 13819 MILWAUKEE, WI 53213

0215

easy GUITAR play along

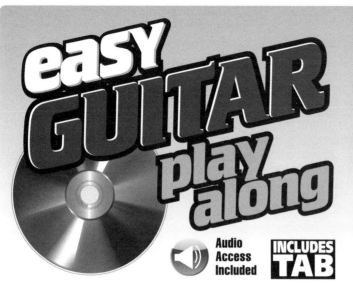

Audio Access Included

INCLUDES TAB

The *Easy Guitar Play Along®* Series features streamlined transcriptions of your favorite songs. Just follow the tab, listen to the audio to hear how the guitar should sound, and then play along using the backing tracks. The CD is playable on any CD player, and is also enhanced to include the Amazing Slowdowner technology so Mac and PC users can adjust the recording to any tempo without changing the pitch!

1. ROCK CLASSICS

Jailbreak • Living After Midnight • Mississippi Queen • Rocks Off • Runnin' Down a Dream • Smoke on the Water • Strutter • Up Around the Bend.

00702560 Book/CD Pack....... $14.99

2. ACOUSTIC TOP HITS

About a Girl • I'm Yours • The Lazy Song • The Scientist • 21 Guns • Upside Down • What I Got • Wonderwall.

00702569 Book/CD Pack $14.99

3. ROCK HITS

All the Small Things • Best of You • Brain Stew (The Godzilla Remix) • Californication • Island in the Sun • Plush • Smells like Teen Spirit • Use Somebody.

00702570 Book/CD Pack $14.99

4. ROCK 'N' ROLL

Blue Suede Shoes • I Get Around • I'm a Believer • Jailhouse Rock • Oh, Pretty Woman • Peggy Sue • Runaway • Wake up Little Susie.

00702572 Book/CD Pack..... $14.99

5. ULTIMATE ACOUSTIC

Against the Wind • Babe, I'm Gonna Leave You • Come Monday • Free Fallin' • Give a Little Bit • Have You Ever Seen the Rain? • New Kid in Town • We Can Work It Out.

00702573 Book/CD Pack........ $14.99

6. CHRISTMAS SONGS

Have Yourself a Merry Little Christmas • A Holly Jolly Christmas • The Little Drummer Boy • Run Rudolph Run • Santa Claus Is Comin' to Town • Silver and Gold • Sleigh Ride • Winter Wonderland.

00101879 Book/CD Pack........ $14.99

7. BLUES SONGS FOR BEGINNERS

Come On (Part 1) • Double Trouble • Gangster of Love • I'm Ready • Let Me Love You Baby • Mary Had a Little Lamb • San-Ho-Zay • T-Bone Shuffle.

00103235 Book/CD Pack $14.99

8. ACOUSTIC SONGS FOR BEGINNERS

Barely Breathing • Drive • Everlong • Good Riddance (Time of Your Life) • Hallelujah • Hey There Delilah • Lake of Fire • Photograph.

00103240 Book/CD Pack..... $14.99

9. ROCK SONGS FOR BEGINNERS

Are You Gonna Be My Girl • Buddy Holly • Everybody Hurts • In Bloom • Otherside • The Rock Show • Santa Monica • When I Come Around.

00103255 Book/CD Pack $14.99

10. GREEN DAY

Basket Case • Boulevard of Broken Dreams • Good Riddance (Time of Your Life) • Holiday • Longview • 21 Guns • Wake Me up When September Ends • When I Come Around.

00122322 Book/CD Pack $14.99

11. NIRVANA

All Apologies • Come As You Are • Heart Shaped Box • Lake of Fire • Lithium • The Man Who Sold the World • Rape Me • Smells like Teen Spirit.

00122325 Book/CD Pack $14.99

12. TAYLOR SWIFT

Fifteen • Love Story • Mean • Picture to Burn • Red • We Are Never Ever Getting Back Together • White Horse • You Belong with Me.

00122326 Book/CD Pack $16.99

14. JIMI HENDRIX – SMASH HITS

All Along the Watchtower • Can You See Me • Crosstown Traffic • Fire • Foxey Lady • Hey Joe • Manic Depression • Purple Haze • Red House • Remember • Stone Free • The Wind Cries Mary.

00130591 Book/ Online Audio........ $24.99

HAL•LEONARD® CORPORATION

7777 W. BLUEMOUND RD. P.O. BOX 13819 MILWAUKEE, WI 53213

www.halleonard.com

Prices, contents, and availability subject to change without notice.

0315